A LITTLE MORE THAN ONE HUNDRED YEARS AGO, a French sculptor named Auguste Bartholdi set out to build the biggest statue in the world as a gift from his country to the United States. The resulting 151-foot-tall Statue of Liberty quickly became an inspiring symbol of freedom and hope on both sides of the Atlantic. The monument in New York harbor is now such a familiar landmark that it is easy to overlook a key fact: Liberty was one of the great engineering feats of the nineteenth century.

Here, in honor of Liberty's centennial in 1986, is a remarkable sketchbook that shows just how the statue was designed and built. Highly detailed drawings—from breathtaking panoramas to helpful cross sections and diagrams—reveal every fascinating step of Liberty's progress; and an illuminating text explains the formidable challenges that the colossal structure presented.

We see Bartholdi, his associates, and hundreds of craftsmen busily at work—making ever larger models…shaping Liberty's copper shell…erecting her giant iron skeleton (whose design by Gustave Eiffel anticipated the structure of skyscrapers)… assembling the statue in Paris…reassembling it in America. Through a skillful combination of words and pictures, the complex building process becomes understandable and totally absorbing.

A tribute to the genius of her creators and to Liberty herself, this magnificently illustrated volume will be pored over and treasured during Liberty's centennial and for years to come.

ILLUSTRATOR'S NOTE

The construction of the Statue of Liberty one hundred years ago was very well documented by photographers of the day; a particularly large collection of photos is now in the Bartholdi Museum in Colmar, France. In addition, Bartholdi himself made a series of small dioramas of the statue's construction, which can still be seen in the National Conservatory of Arts and Crafts in Paris. The illustrations in this book are closely based on these sources, but they are not mere copies. For the sake of clarity, I have added extra details from other sources; shifted perspectives; and, when a clear historical record was not available, imagined what must have happened. For their help on the illustrations I would particularly like to thank: Mr. J. Burger, Curator of the Bartholdi Museum; Miss Frederique Desvergnes, National Technical Museum, Paris; and Mr. Pierre Tissier, engineer, Paris.

HUCK SCARRY

OVERLEAF: New York harbor soon after Liberty's unveiling in 1886 (seen from the southern tip of Manhattan).

How they built the STATUE OF LIBERTY

How they built the STATUE

by MARY J. SHAPIRO

RANDOM HOUSE · NEW YORK

OF LIBERTY

illustrated by HUCK SCARRY

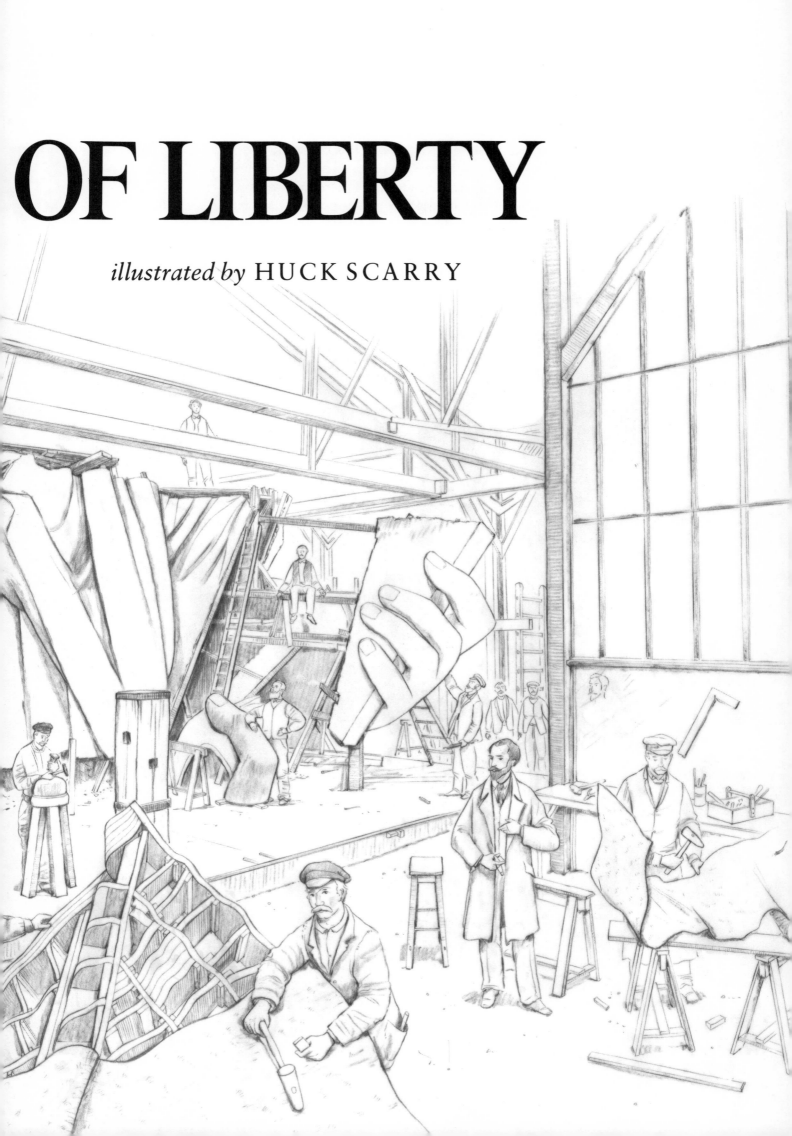

To Michael and Eben

AUTHOR'S NOTE

Most of the original documents of Liberty's construction have been lost, so a thorough study of the statue—with new drawings, plans, and diagrams—had to be made during the course of her recent restoration. The architects, engineers, and artisans who carried out that work have not only succeeded in repairing a national treasure but, through their research, have also restored a significant part of Liberty's history. The step-by-step descriptions in this book of the methods used to build the statue are derived in large part from conversations I had with members of the restoration team.

I owe special thanks to John Robbins, Historical Architect for the National Park Service, and Jean Wiart of Les Metalliers Champenois for sharing with me their expert knowledge of the statue and how it was built. I learned a great deal from visiting the workshop set up at the base of Liberty's pedestal, where Mr. Wiart and fellow craftsmen rebuilt the torch employing the same techniques Bartholdi used a century earlier. Philip Kleiner of Lehrer/McGovern Inc. and Thierry Despont, Associate Architect for the Restoration of the Statue of Liberty, also offered constructive advice, and Mr. Despont provided me with architectural diagrams as well.

Nineteenth-century sources which were consulted include Bartholdi's own account, *The Statue of Liberty Enlightening the World described by the Sculptor Bartholdi* (ed. A.T. Rice, New York, 1885); *"La Statue de la Liberte l'eclairant la monde"* by C. Talansier, published in *Le Genie Civil* on August 1, 1883; "The Bartholdi Statue" published in *St. Nicholas Magazine* in July of 1884; and several articles in *Scientific American* published in 1885 and 1886; as well as accounts in many other periodicals of the day. Recently published books that were helpful include Marvin Trachtenberg's *The Statue of Liberty* (1976) and Andre Gschaedler's *True Light on the Statue of Liberty and its Creator* (1966).

I am indebted to my editor, Eugenia Fanelli, for her invaluable guidance and help.

Most of all, I am deeply grateful to my husband, Barry, for his constant and loving encouragement and support.

MARY J. SHAPIRO

The publisher is grateful to John Robbins, Historical Architect for the National Park Service, and Jean Wiart of Les Metalliers Champenois for reading the manuscript for accuracy.

BOOK DESIGN: *Jos. Trautwein/Bentwood Studio*

Library of Congress Cataloging in Publication Data: Shapiro, Mary J. How they built the Statue of Liberty. SUMMARY: Panoramas, cross sections, and diagrams provide a detailed portrayal of the construction of the Statue of Liberty, one of the nineteenth century's greatest engineering feats. 1. Statue of Liberty (New York, N.Y.) [1. Statue of Liberty (New York, N.Y.) 2. National monuments. 3. Statues] I. Scarry, Huck, ill. II. Title. F128.64.L6S48 1985 974.7'1 85-42720 ISBN: 0-394-86957-5 (trade); 0-394-96957-X (lib. bdg.)

Manufactured in the United States of America 1 2 3 4 5 6 7 8 9 0

Auguste Bartholdi (seated, far left) and Edouard de Laboulaye (standing), the originators of the Liberty project.

How it all began...

ON OCTOBER 28, 1886, Americans celebrated the unveiling of the Statue of Liberty with enormous enthusiasm—and awe. Few of the people watching had ever seen anything so big. Liberty was the tallest statue in the world. Standing 305 feet high atop her pedestal on Bedloe's Island in New York Bay, she was taller than any building then in Manhattan.

Since that day, Liberty's height has been topped many times over by New York's skyscrapers. Yet, from her dramatic site at America's gateway, she still commands the affection of people all over the world. Countless ocean travelers, arriving immigrants, and American soldiers and sailors going off to war have been heartened by the sight of her proudly held torch of freedom. Over the years Liberty has become so popular as a symbol of America that it is easy to forget that the statue was made in France. It was, in fact, a gift from the people of France to the people of the United States.

The idea for building a statue dedicated to liberty first came up at a dinner party in France in 1865. The host was Edouard de Laboulaye, a famous French historian and a great admirer of America. The after-dinner conversation turned to the special friendship between France and the United States that had existed since the American Revolution. At that time France alone had sent aid to the colonists fighting for their freedom from England. Laboulaye suggested that, in memory of this, the former allies should jointly build a monument to American independence. His words deeply moved one of his guests, a young sculptor named Frédéric-Auguste Bartholdi.

Bartholdi first went to Egypt in 1856 to see the pyramids, the Sphinx, and these granite images of the Pharaohs. The giant works of art made him want to build something equally grand one day.

Bartholdi was born in 1834 in the little town of Colmar in Alsace, a province in eastern France. But he grew up in Paris, where he later studied art. When he was only 19 years old, he opened his own sculpture studio. He was very successful and his work was in constant demand.

Bartholdi had a passion for grand-scale works of art. He lived in a new technological age that was obsessed with building bigger and bigger things—giant steam engines, mammoth ocean-going vessels, and amazingly long bridges. Bartholdi was caught up in this modern enthusiasm, but he found his artistic inspiration in the huge old stone sculptures of Egypt.

In 1867 he met Ismā'īl Pasha, the new Egyptian ruler. He tried to interest Ismā'īl in building a monumental lighthouse at the entrance of the Suez Canal, which was then under construction. When Ismā'īl finally decided against the project, Bartholdi looked around for another opportunity to build a gigantic sculpture. Now Laboulaye's idea for a monument to liberty came to mind.

Bartholdi made his first designs and models for Liberty in 1870, naming the statue "Liberty Enlightening the World." At the time he had no idea how his statue would be built or who would pay for it. But the one hundredth anniversary of America's declaration of independence was just six years away. It was the natural occasion for erecting a monument. Bartholdi had no time to waste.

Later that year the Franco-Prussian War broke out. It lasted only five months, but when it was over France was forced to surrender the province of Alsace—Bartholdi's birthplace—to Germany. The loss of his homeland made Bartholdi fiercely determined to build his statue to liberty. As soon as the war was over, he planned a trip to the United States. Laboulaye encouraged Bartholdi to go there and drum up support for the Liberty project.

Bartholdi arrived in New York in June of 1871. As his ship steamed into New York's harbor, he spotted Bedloe's Island, a tiny parcel of land in the middle of the bay. Bartholdi knew at once that it was the perfect site for his statue.

From New York, Bartholdi traveled across the whole country—even taking the recently completed transcontinental railroad all the way to San Francisco. He met many important Americans, including President Ulysses S. Grant. Bartholdi wrote to Laboulaye that the Americans were very enthusiastic about jointly raising a monument to liberty. But, he added, it was up to France to make the first move.

France, however, was still in a state of turmoil after the war, and Laboulaye was busy with other things. But three years later, in 1874, he organized the Franco-American Union to raise money for building the Statue of Liberty. Meanwhile, friends in America promised to provide the pedestal.

By 1875 Bartholdi had completed his final model of Liberty—Liberty as we know her today—holding aloft a torch of freedom and striding forward out of the shackles and chains of tyranny. In her left arm she carries a tablet inscribed with the date of American independence, July 4, 1776, in Roman numerals. On her head she wears a crown with seven rays, representing the seven seas and the seven continents of the world.

The construction of the Statue of Liberty presented an enormous challenge. No sculpture as large as Liberty had ever been attempted before. When completed, she would stand 151 feet tall. Most of the sculpture techniques Bartholdi planned to use were centuries old, but they had never before been employed on so great a scale.

Liberty would be fashioned from hundreds of thin plates of copper fitted together like a gigantic three-dimensional jigsaw puzzle. The copper shell would be no thicker than 3/32 inch, but all together the plates would weigh 100 tons. The shell would need a sturdy interior support to keep it from buckling under its own weight and collapsing. Bartholdi called in France's foremost engineer, Alexandre Gustave Eiffel, to design a framework.

Eiffel came up with an ingenious scheme for a freestanding iron skeleton of exceptional strength. It could bear the entire weight of the giant shell—the first such load-bearing framework ever. (American architects came up with a similar skeleton

In its structure, Liberty had some similarities to the giant statue of Saint Charles Borromeo near Arona, Italy, which Bartholdi visited in 1869. Standing 76 feet tall—114 feet counting the pedestal—Borromeo was made of beaten copper plates attached to iron hooks in a core of stone.

Bartholdi's design for a lighthouse on the Suez Canal. Bartholdi hotly denied that the Statue of Liberty was in any way derived from this design, despite the two projects' obvious similarity. (The ship has been added to this copy of Bartholdi's sketch to give an idea of the statue's size.)

Liberty's torch was one of the most popular and unusual displays at the Philadelphia Centennial Exhibition in 1876. A narrow ladder inside the arm enabled hardy fairgoers to clamber up to the balcony around the copper flame.

A few years after the Philadelphia Centennial, New York City newspaper publisher Joseph Pulitzer became the most energetic of the fund-raisers for Liberty's pedestal.

independently when they invented skyscrapers just a few years later.) Together, Bartholdi's vision and Eiffel's expertise make the Statue of Liberty one of the most astonishing feats of art and engineering in the world.

The fund-raising for the statue began on November 6, 1875, at a grand banquet in Paris. By the end of the year $40,000 had been contributed to the Franco-American Union. Bartholdi and a crew of craftsmen set to work immediately. They could not possibly complete the entire monument for the American centennial in 1876. But Liberty's torch was finished in time to go on display in Philadelphia in October. Next Bartholdi oversaw construction of Liberty's head in the huge Paris workshop of Gaget, Gauthier & Co. This firm specialized in making large-scale works of art out of metal. A team of twelve horses pulled the finished head through the city streets to the Paris Universal Exposition, a world's fair held in 1878.

As president of the Franco-American Union, Laboulaye worked hard to raise money for Bartholdi's work. The fund-raising campaign was widely publicized. Generous contributions came in from organizations and more than 100,000 citizens all over France. Bartholdi contributed $20,000 of his own money as well as all of his work on the statue. He also made 200 small models of Liberty for the Franco-American Union to sell. By July of 1880, $400,000, covering the full cost of the statue, had been raised.

Meanwhile, a crew of carpenters, sculptors, and coppersmiths were building Liberty's copper body from the toes up. In 1881 ironworkers started to erect the statue's iron skeleton in the tiny yard outside the Gaget Gauthier workshop. Over the next two and a half years Liberty gradually rose above the rooftops of Paris. In August of 1883 workers hoisted the head into place. A few months later they installed the right arm and torch, which had been returned from America, and Liberty was finished.

The French formally presented their colossus to the Americans on July 4, 1884, in a ceremony at the workyard. Sadly, the elderly Laboulaye did not live to see this event.

Now it was the Americans' turn to complete their share of the project, that is, to build a pedestal for Liberty. A fund-raising group called the American Committee had been active in New York for several years. Its first campaign, in 1881, brought in just enough money to begin work. Bedloe's Island was chosen as the site for the statue, as Bartholdi had wished. The committee asked Richard Morris Hunt, one of America's most fashionable architects, to design a pedestal in 1882. The following year the committee named General Charles P. Stone as chief engineer in charge of the pedestal's construction. Work started with a simple ground-breaking ceremony on April 18, 1883.

The estimated cost of building the foundation and pedestal and raising the statue when it arrived from Paris was $250,000. New appeals went out all across the United States. The American Committee sponsored fairs, theatrical events, and benefit concerts. It sold statuettes of Liberty.

For a small fee, visitors could climb the spiral staircase inside Liberty's crown to enjoy a fine view of the Paris Exposition in 1878. The admission money helped to pay for the statue's construction.

The committee also organized an art and literary show for which Emma Lazarus, a young poet, wrote her famous sonnet "The New Colossus"—a poem that was eventually to be displayed inside the pedestal. Lazarus gave the statue a powerful meaning for immigrants seeking a new life of freedom and opportunity in America:

"Keep, ancient lands, your storied pomp!" cries she
With silent lips. "Give me your tired, your poor,
Your huddled masses yearning to breathe free,
The wretched refuse of your teeming shore.
Send these, the homeless, tempest-tost to me,
I lift my lamp beside the golden door!"

But somehow the committee's fund-raising efforts failed to inspire widespread support. Wealthy New Yorkers contributed, but not nearly enough of them—and not nearly enough money. In October 1884—three months after the statue was officially handed over in Paris—the American Committee had only $2,000 left in its treasury and was forced to halt all work on the pedestal.

Liberty stood in Paris until the following January. Then, even though the pedestal was far from complete, an impatient Bartholdi ordered his workmen to start taking the statue down and packing it for shipment to America. Liberty's future looked very uncertain. The embarrassing situation in America dragged on for two more months until Joseph Pulitzer, publisher and editor of the New York *World,* came to the rescue in March 1885.

The sum of $100,000 was needed to complete Liberty's pedestal. To raise the money, Pulitzer wrote a lead editorial in his newspaper practically every day for the next five months. He lambasted the rich as tight-fisted, mean, and stingy. He appealed directly to the people to give whatever they could—no matter how small the amount—to pay for the pedestal's construction.

As the editorials continued, people sent in their pennies, nickels, dimes, and dollars—young office boys, struggling artists, recent immigrants, schoolchildren, the poor and the elderly. By May work on the pedestal could begin once again. On August 11 the *World* triumphantly announced that $100,000 had been contributed by more than 120,000 patriotic citizens. At long last Liberty was assured a proper home in America.

Building the Statue of Liberty was a huge venture for its time. It demanded the vision, ingenuity, and dedication of many people. Bartholdi devoted 16 years to the project, and Laboulaye, Eiffel, Hunt, Stone, and Pulitzer also played major roles. But planning and fund-raising were only one part of the story. The actual construction of the mammoth statue was a highly complex process, requiring the skills of hundreds of craftsmen. Here, step by step, is how the statue went up.

While the Americans struggled to top off their pedestal fund, Liberty stood complete for more than a year in the workshop yard in Paris.

The first models

Auguste Bartholdi began designing his statue in 1870 by making numerous drawings and then small clay models. There were many questions to answer: What should Liberty look like? How should she be dressed? What should she hold in her hands?

The sculptor's final design was in the form of a 4-foot-high clay model. It was enthusiastically approved by the Franco-American Union, the organizers of the Liberty project, in 1875.

Bartholdi then built a series of increasingly larger plaster models. With each new model he made little changes in the design so that the statue looked right in its larger size.

The second model stood about 9½ feet tall—$\frac{1}{16}$ the height of the 151-foot-tall statue that Bartholdi planned. The third model was four times bigger than the second—about 38 feet high. It was called the quarter-size model because it was one quarter (¼) the size of the final statue.

The 4-foot model

The ⅟₁₆-size model

It has often been said that Bartholdi modeled Liberty's face to look like his mother's. Photographs show that there was actually little resemblance between the two except perhaps in the stern expression.

Bartholdi studied the ¼-size model very carefully. The next model—a full-size one in plaster—would be built in sections. So the ¼-size model was Bartholdi's last chance to see the planned statue in one piece and make any changes in the design.

The 38-foot-high ¼-size model was so big that it had to be stored outdoors. A special shed was built to hold it in the Paris workyard of Gaget, Gauthier & Co., the metal-working shop where the finished statue was to be constructed of copper.

The ¼-size model

17

Building the full-size model

For the final, full-scale model of Liberty, the craftsmen at Gaget, Gauthier & Co. had to enlarge each section of the ¼-size model with absolute precision. Here is how they did it:

First they built a special measuring frame whose base and top were exactly the same size. The base was marked off with a grid pattern and the top was marked off at the same intervals.

A section of the ¼-size model was placed on the base. Horizontal lines were drawn around the model, and each line was given a Roman numeral. Along each of these lines the craftsmen marked reference points with short vertical strokes about three inches apart. They were especially careful to include major points like the tip of the nose and the center of the eyes.

Then, using rulers and plumb lines, the craftsmen took three measurements for each reference point—the width and depth (meaning the distance in from each side of the frame) and the height. The measurements for all the reference points of each level were plotted on separate sheets of graph paper. Now the craftsmen had an outline for the shape of the ¼-size model at each level and were ready to build the full-size model.

level 8

7

6

5

4

3

2

1

The full-size model and the statue itself had to be built in sections because Liberty was simply too big to handle in one piece. Bartholdi first built the right arm and torch so they could go on display at the Philadelphia Centennial Exhibition of 1876. Next he built the head for display at the Paris Universal Exposition of 1878. The rest of the statue was built afterward in eight separate layers plus a connecting piece of arm.

A plumb line consists of a lead weight on a string. It hangs absolutely straight, allowing the worker to make accurate measurements along it.

¼ size

A craftsman measuring a reference point at level V of the head.

1

2

1. Next to the measuring frame for the ¼-size model, the craftsmen built another frame that was exactly four times as large. The grid pattern on its base was the same as on the smaller frame's base—except, of course, four times bigger. Beginning with the bottom of the model, the workers looked at the outline on the graph paper and transferred the marks for the reference points to the corresponding positions on the larger grid.

2. Once the bottom level of the model was outlined on the larger grid, the workers could begin building a framework for the section. This framework, called an armature, was started off with wooden beams.

3. Using the graphs of the different levels as guides, the workers built up the armature. They covered the beams with small strips of wood called lath. Then each reference point on the smaller model was indicated with a protruding nailhead on the full-size model. Next the lath was plastered over to the top of the nailheads.

4. When the rough plaster dried, the craftsmen carved it with rasps and files to make the full-size model as finely sculpted as the ¼-size model.

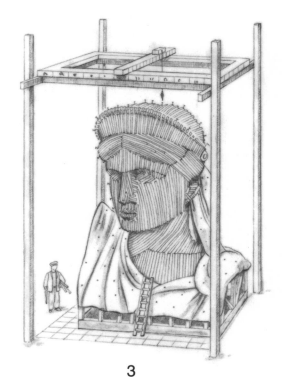

3

¼ size   full size   4

As the fine sculpting proceeded, each point on the full-size model was checked against the smaller model again and again. The copy had to be exact. Otherwise Liberty would be misshapen and the sections of the finished statue would not fit together properly.

Building the full-size model required endless amounts of measuring—and endless care and patience on the part of the workers. Each reference point had to be measured a minimum of six times—three times (height, width, depth) on the ¼-size model and three times on the full-size model. Since each section of the statue had an average of 1,500 reference points, at least 9,000 separate measurements were required per section. Double-checking added many more.

Much of the fine sculpting still had to be done by eye. Plaster copies of important details of the ¼-size model were hung on the scaffolding around the larger model so the sculptors could refer to them easily.

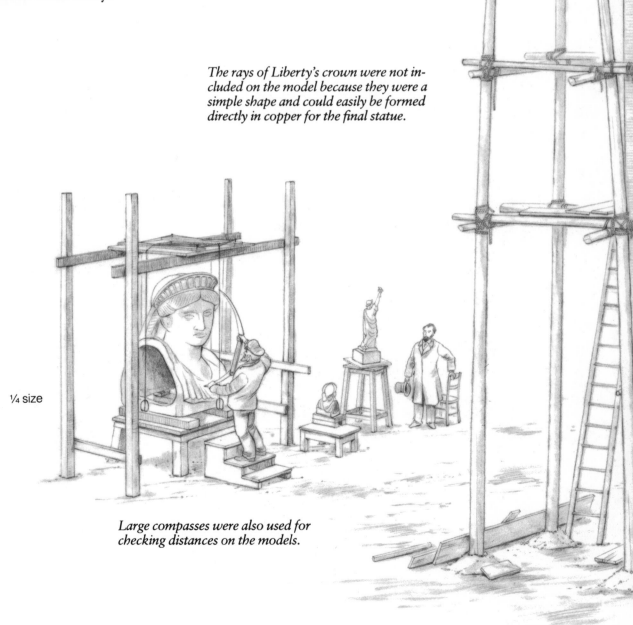

The rays of Liberty's crown were not included on the model because they were a simple shape and could easily be formed directly in copper for the final statue.

¼ size

Large compasses were also used for checking distances on the models.

full size

Liberty's head and shoulders were about 30 feet high in their full size.

After Liberty's arm and torch and head were completed, Bartholdi's crew began to build the full-size model of her body. They started at the bottom and worked up, layer by layer. This picture shows the seventh level—Liberty's left arm and part of her tablet.

The eight layers of Liberty's body were each about 30 feet wide and 12 feet high.

There was enough room inside Gaget Gauthier's huge shed to work on four sections of the full-size model at a time. The ¼-size models of the sections under construction were placed in the center of the workshop, where they could easily be seen and copied.

Workers mixed up batches of plaster in large wooden troughs. Then they carried the wet plaster to the worksites in shallow pans.

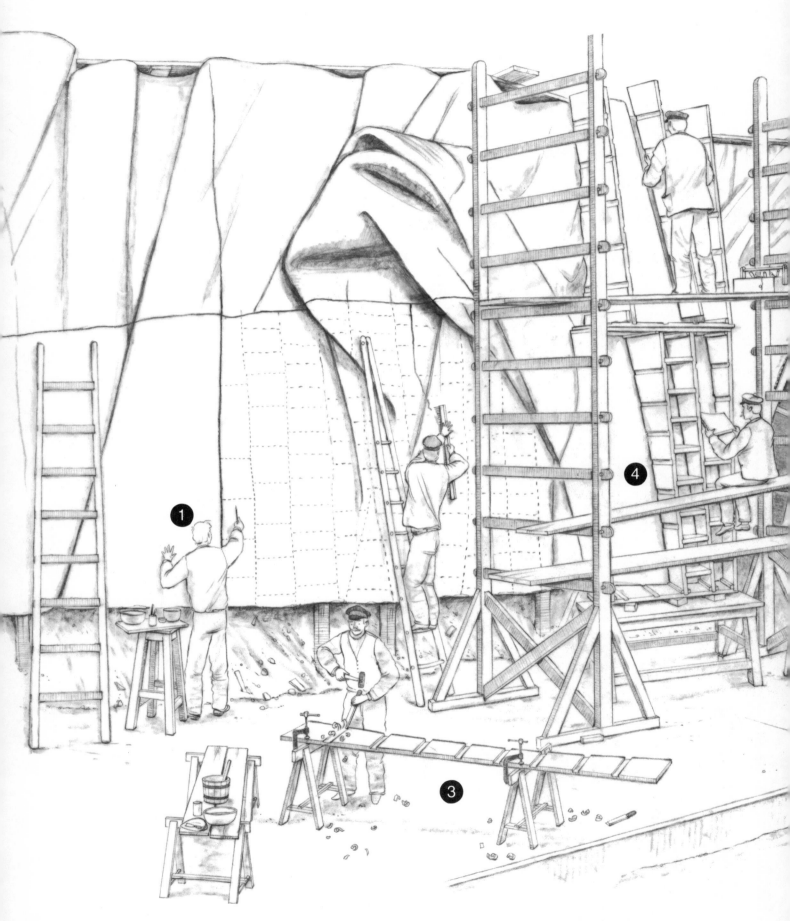

To build the molds, the carpenters first marked off rectangles on the full-size plaster model. Within each rectangle they marked where individual boards should go (**1**). For each mold, long boards were cut and shaped to follow the contours of the plaster (**2**). Grooves were cut in the long boards to hold

Building the wooden molds

After a section of the full-size model was finished, the next step was to duplicate its form in copper. Bartholdi had designed his statue to be built from thin sheets of the metal. His men, however, could not simply put a sheet against the plaster model and hammer it to the same shape. The plaster would have shattered. The coppersmiths needed a hard surface to hammer against. So carpenters built wooden molds whose surface was the exact reverse of the model's surface. Where the plaster model curved outward, for example, the wooden mold curved inward.

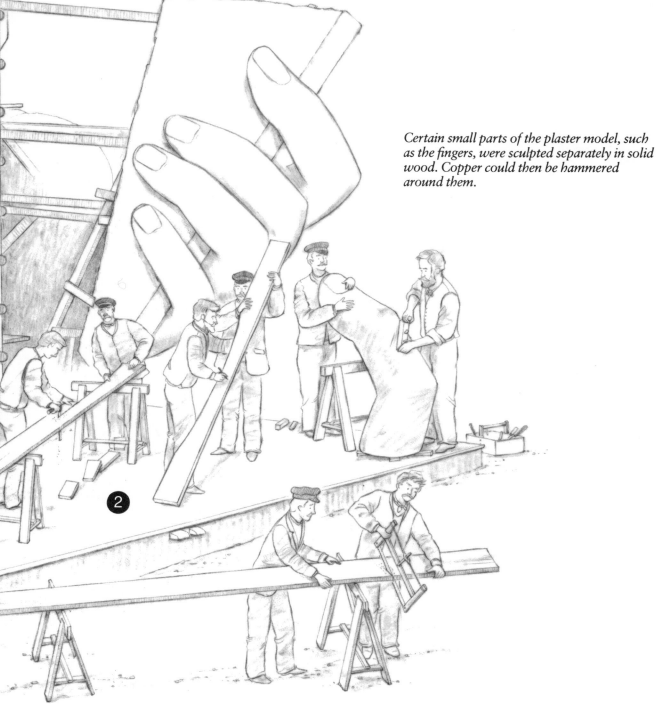

Certain small parts of the plaster model, such as the fingers, were sculpted separately in solid wood. Copper could then be hammered around them.

crosspieces like shelves (**3**). The long boards were assembled in a frame against the plaster, and the short "shelves" were inserted. These shorter boards were also shaped to fit closely against the plaster (**4**). Where there were deep curves, the rectangular molds were built in sections for easy removal.

The more complex the plaster surface, the more wooden crosspieces were inserted in the mold. The usual open framework would not have reproduced the shape of the plaster surface in enough detail. So the carpenters created a solid wooden surface to hammer the copper against.

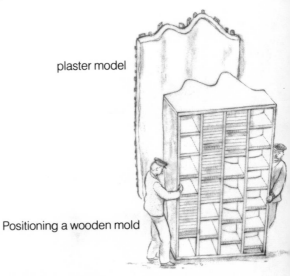

plaster model

Positioning a wooden mold

Soon an entire area of the plaster model's surface was covered with wooden molds. Each was then pulled away from the model and placed on its back, so that the reversed copy of the statue's surface faced upward.

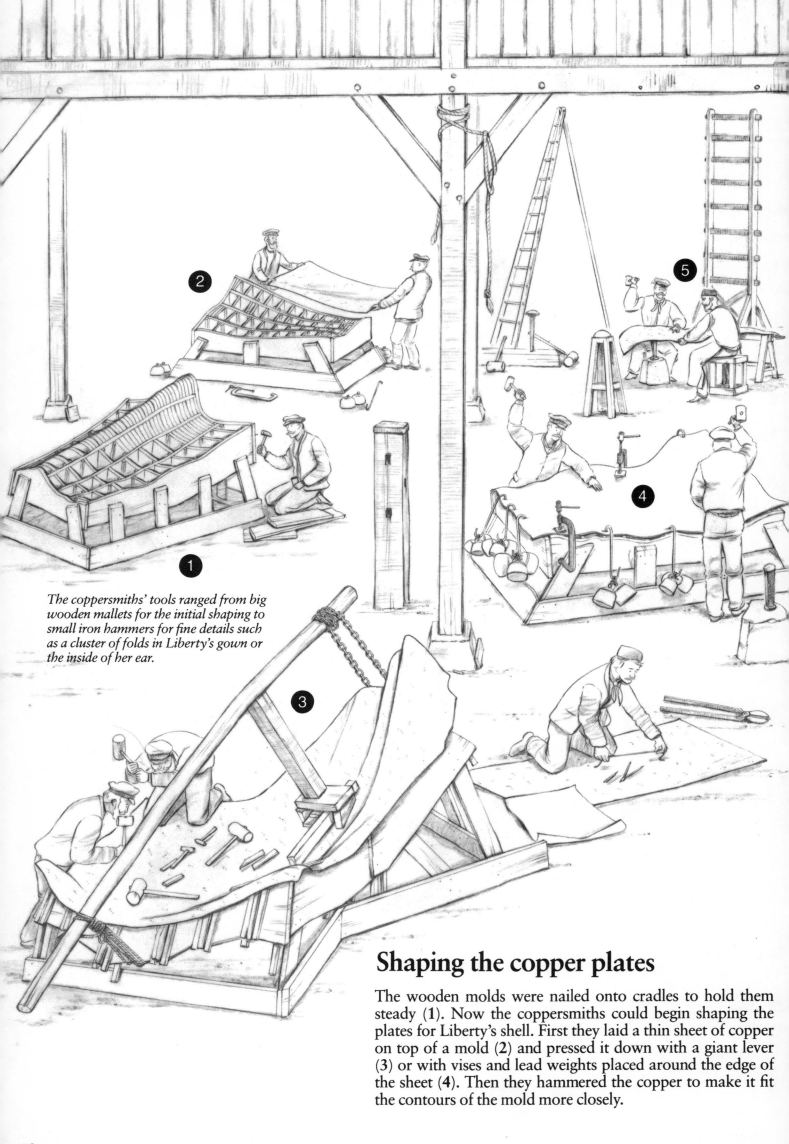

The coppersmiths' tools ranged from big wooden mallets for the initial shaping to small iron hammers for fine details such as a cluster of folds in Liberty's gown or the inside of her ear.

Shaping the copper plates

The wooden molds were nailed onto cradles to hold them steady (**1**). Now the coppersmiths could begin shaping the plates for Liberty's shell. First they laid a thin sheet of copper on top of a mold (**2**) and pressed it down with a giant lever (**3**) or with vises and lead weights placed around the edge of the sheet (**4**). Then they hammered the copper to make it fit the contours of the mold more closely.

The metal shell of the statue had to be as thin and light in weight as possible—because the statue was so big and because it was to be shipped to America. Bartholdi chose to make the shell from copper, which is relatively light and was not very expensive at that time. Most of the copper for the statue was, in fact, donated by a French manufacturer of cookware.

Most metal statues are made by casting—melting down the metal and pouring it into a mold. This method makes a shell from $1/4$ to $1/2$ inch thick. But Bartholdi chose instead to hammer sheets of copper into shape, a method that produces a much thinner shell. He used sheets that were a mere $3/32$ inch thick, about the same thickness as a silver dollar. This cut down not only the cost of material but also the weight. Even so, the entire shell of 350 plates weighs 100 tons.

Sometimes the coppersmiths did not need a wooden mold to guide their work. For the simpler plates, they would instead shape the copper by eye, hammering it against an anvil or a mandrel. A mandrel is like an anvil on top of a long stake, held upright in a large block of wood (5).

Hammering metal makes it harder but also more brittle. To keep the copper sheet from cracking, workers would often remove it from its mold or mandrel and heat it up with a long-handled blowtorch (6). The metal softened from the heat and became easier to work with. This process is call annealing.

Because the wooden molds were a reverse impression of the statue's surface, the coppersmiths were actually shaping Liberty's shell from the inside. On each copper sheet, the surface that they worked on would end up inside the statue. This method of sculpting—hammering a thin sheet of metal on its inside surface to form an image or shape on the outside—is known as repoussé. (The French term means "push back," but a better description is "push out.") It produces a smoothly shaped outer surface and is actually easier than working directly on the outside surface of the metal. Repoussé is a very old technique, first used in ancient Greece. The craftsmen at Gaget Gauthier were experts at it.

A finishing touch was to bevel, or slant, the edges of some of the copper plates by filing them down. The plates would then be fastened together by small (⅕ inch wide) copper rivets (**1**). They were spaced about an inch apart in holes drilled all around the edges of each plate. Beveled edges made the seam between two plates almost invisible. It was especially important to have smooth, flawless seams on the arm and torch and on the head. These two pieces of the statue were each displayed at a world's fair and could be seen close up.

Beveling was difficult to do and very time-consuming. So the coppersmiths often used other joints. Sometimes they butted two plates together, joining them with an extra strip of copper riveted to the back (**2**). The plates in Liberty's face were held together this way, except in her cheeks. There the plates were dovetailed (**3**) and then soldered together—held together by melting a thin strip of metal over the joint. Dovetailing was also used to patch damaged plates in spots where the coppersmiths had hammered the metal too thin or had punched through it.

For the body of the statue, the plates were simply overlapped and joined with a single row of rivets (**4**). The edge of the upper plate was always on the outside so that rain would run off the statue. Most of these overlapped seams are hidden in the deep folds of Liberty's robes.

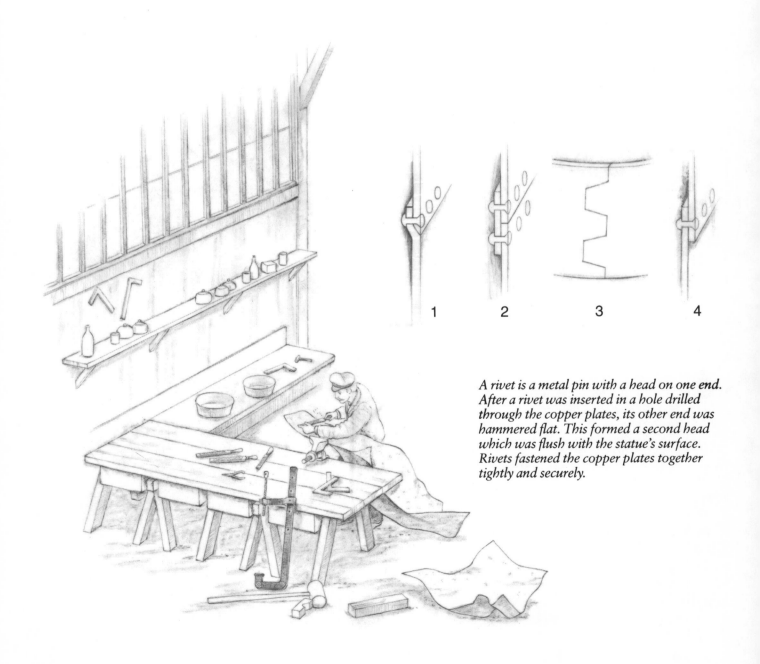

1   2   3   4

A rivet is a metal pin with a head on one end. After a rivet was inserted in a hole drilled through the copper plates, its other end was hammered flat. This formed a second head which was flush with the statue's surface. Rivets fastened the copper plates together tightly and securely.

The last step in making the copper shell was to forge iron straps to fit the exact shape of each plate. The 2-inch-wide straps, called ribs, were attached two or more to a plate in horizontal and vertical positions. The strong iron ribs would keep the relatively soft copper from losing its shape over the years. And when the entire shell was put together, the ribs would form a network of support.

The iron ribs could not be allowed to touch the copper plates directly. If the two metals touched in the moist salt air of New York harbor, a battery would be created: a tiny electrical current would flow between the metals and slowly eat the iron away. To prevent such corrosion, the iron ribs were heavily shellacked. Also, when the ribs were attached to the plates, strips of asbestos were inserted between the two metals to keep them apart.

Work proceeded in round-robin fashion from one section of the statue to the next. Soon all stages of construction were going on at once—sculpting plaster enlargements, building wooden molds, hammering copper plates. As many as 50 craftsmen worked in the shop at a time. After a section of Liberty was completed in copper, its plaster model was demolished to make room for building another section. And so the work continued until all eight levels of the statue's body were finished, from the toes up to the shoulders.

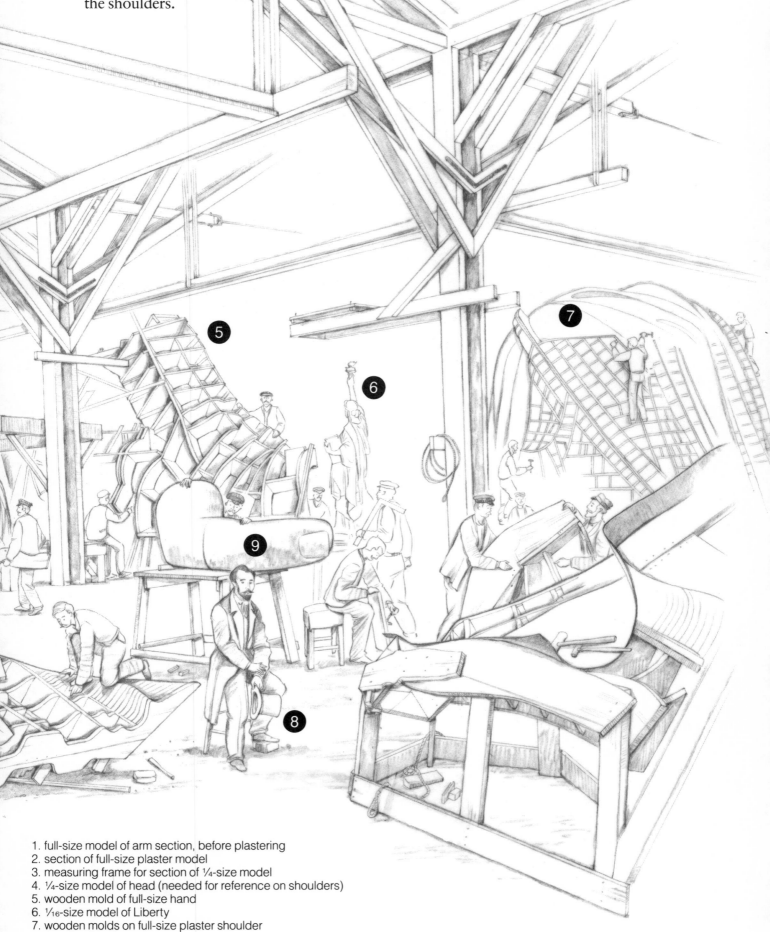

1. full-size model of arm section, before plastering
2. section of full-size plaster model
3. measuring frame for section of ¼-size model
4. ¼-size model of head (needed for reference on shoulders)
5. wooden mold of full-size hand
6. ¹⁄₁₆-size model of Liberty
7. wooden molds on full-size plaster shoulder
8. Auguste Bartholdi
9. copper finger
10. copper sheet on wooden mold

Liberty's skeleton

Outside the workshop a different kind of construction was going on. In 1881—well before the upper levels of Liberty's body were built—workers started to erect the huge wrought-iron skeleton for the statue. Liberty's shell was not nearly rigid enough to stand up on its own. The statue was so tall and its shell so thin that it needed a strong interior framework to support it.

Up till then, large metal sculptures had usually been supported by a central core of wood or stone. This method was not practical for a statue the size of Liberty. An early plan for her support was to attach the copper plates to an iron frame and then fill the statue up to her hips with sand. The sand would keep her from toppling over in a high wind.

Auguste Bartholdi with Gustave Eiffel (standing), the brilliant engineer who designed Liberty's skeleton. In 1889 Eiffel would build the giant iron Eiffel Tower in Paris. At 984 feet, it was the tallest structure in the world until the Chrysler Building in New York City was completed in 1930.

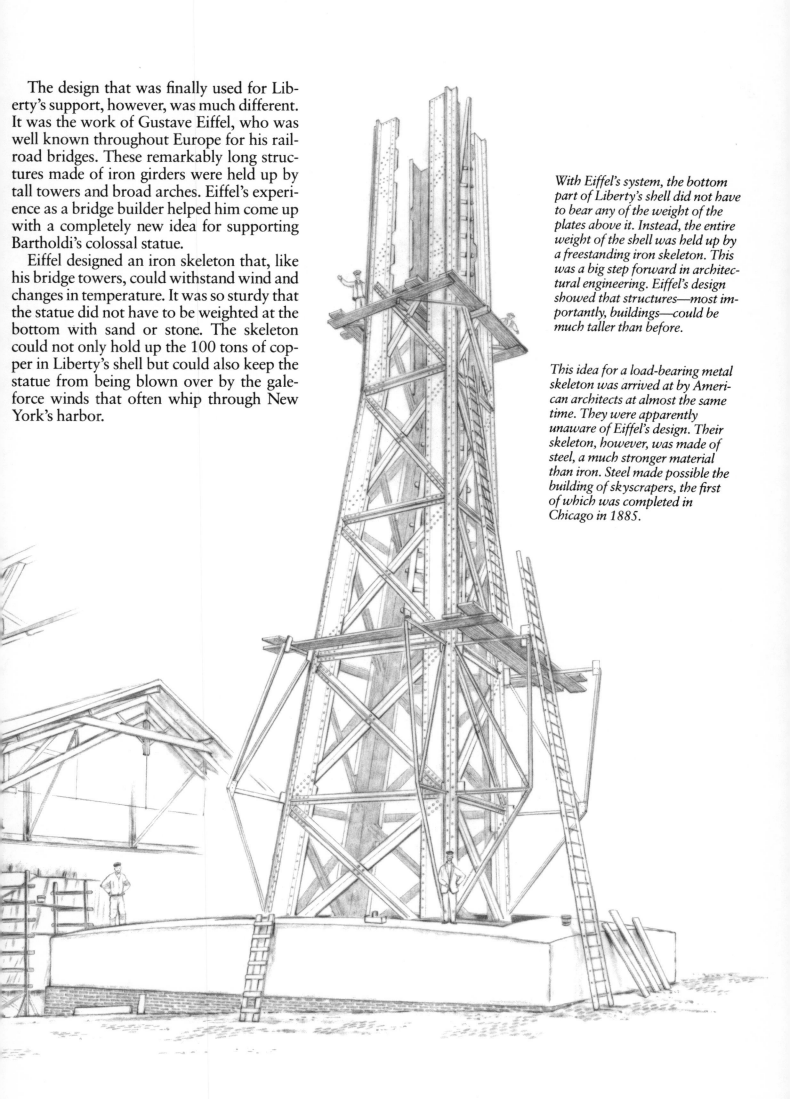

The design that was finally used for Liberty's support, however, was much different. It was the work of Gustave Eiffel, who was well known throughout Europe for his railroad bridges. These remarkably long structures made of iron girders were held up by tall towers and broad arches. Eiffel's experience as a bridge builder helped him come up with a completely new idea for supporting Bartholdi's colossal statue.

Eiffel designed an iron skeleton that, like his bridge towers, could withstand wind and changes in temperature. It was so sturdy that the statue did not have to be weighted at the bottom with sand or stone. The skeleton could not only hold up the 100 tons of copper in Liberty's shell but could also keep the statue from being blown over by the gale-force winds that often whip through New York's harbor.

With Eiffel's system, the bottom part of Liberty's shell did not have to bear any of the weight of the plates above it. Instead, the entire weight of the shell was held up by a freestanding iron skeleton. This was a big step forward in architectural engineering. Eiffel's design showed that structures—most importantly, buildings—could be much taller than before.

This idea for a load-bearing metal skeleton was arrived at by American architects at almost the same time. They were apparently unaware of Eiffel's design. Their skeleton, however, was made of steel, a much stronger material than iron. Steel made possible the building of skyscrapers, the first of which was completed in Chicago in 1885.

35

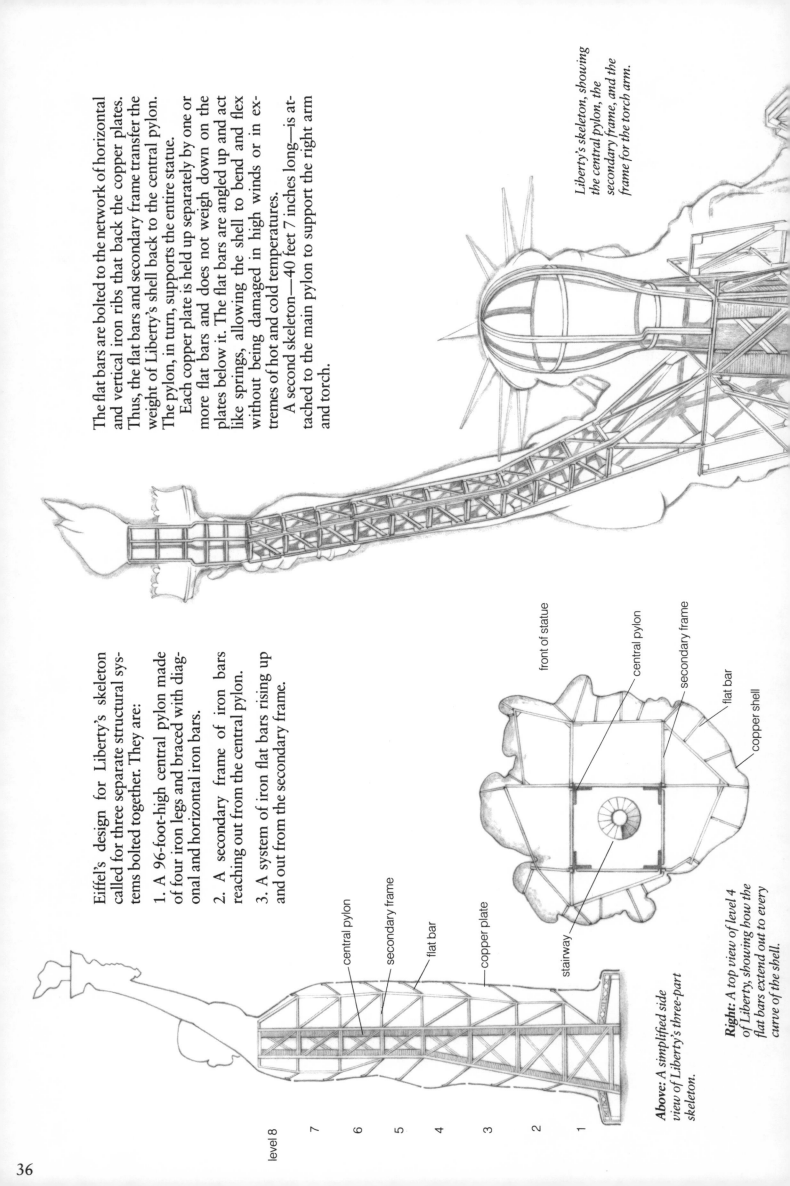

The flat bars are bolted to the network of horizontal and vertical iron ribs that back the copper plates. Thus, the flat bars and secondary frame transfer the weight of Liberty's shell back to the central pylon. The pylon, in turn, supports the entire statue.

Each copper plate is held up separately by one or more flat bars and does not weigh down on the plates below it. The flat bars are angled up and act like springs, allowing the shell to bend and flex without being damaged in high winds or in extremes of hot and cold temperatures.

A second skeleton—40 feet 7 inches long—is attached to the main pylon to support the right arm and torch.

Liberty's skeleton, showing the central pylon, the secondary frame, and the frame for the torch arm.

Eiffel's design for Liberty's skeleton called for three separate structural systems bolted together. They are:

1. A 96-foot-high central pylon made of four iron legs and braced with diagonal and horizontal iron bars.

2. A secondary frame of iron bars reaching out from the central pylon.

3. A system of iron flat bars rising up and out from the secondary frame.

central pylon

secondary frame

flat bar

copper plate

Above: A simplified side view of Liberty's three-part skeleton.

level 8
7
6
5
4
3
2
1

front of statue

central pylon

secondary frame

flat bar

copper shell

stairway

Right: A top view of level 4 of Liberty, showing how the flat bars extend out to every curve of the shell.

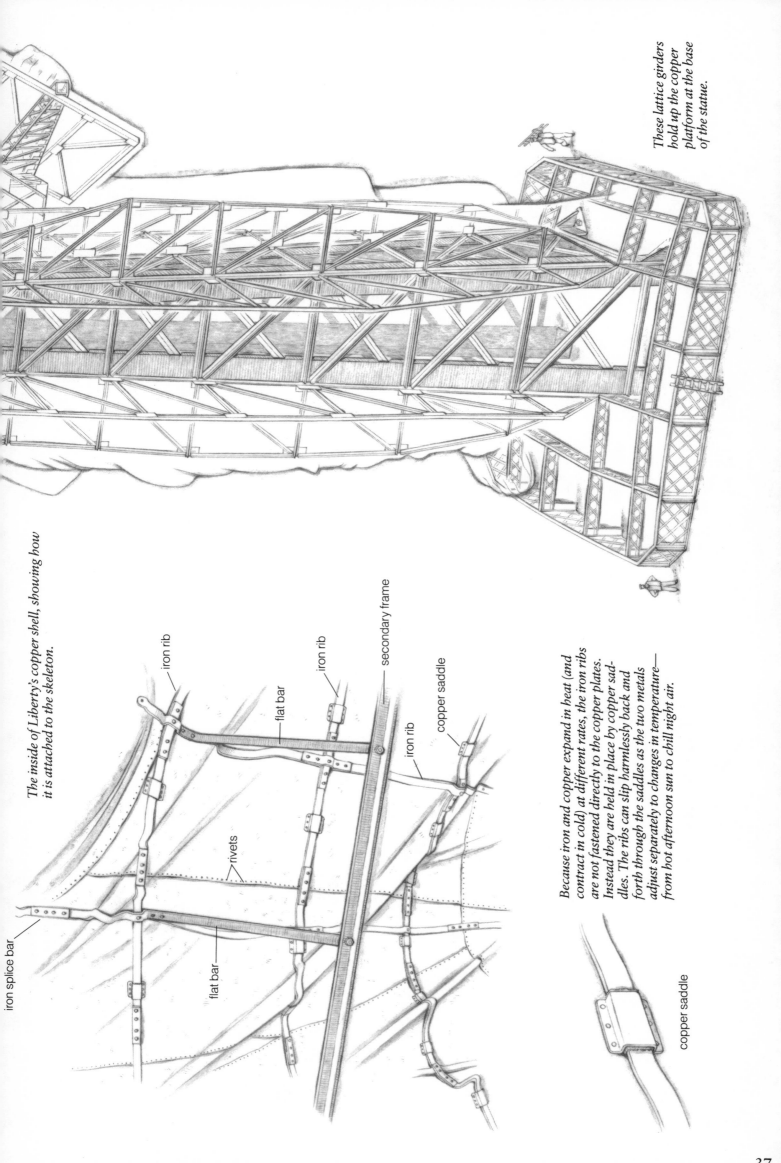

These lattice girders hold up the copper platform at the base of the statue.

The inside of Liberty's copper shell, showing how it is attached to the skeleton.

iron splice bar

iron rib

flat bar

iron rib

rivets

flat bar

secondary frame

iron rib

copper saddle

Because iron and copper expand in heat (and contract in cold) at different rates, the iron ribs are not fastened directly to the copper plates. Instead they are held in place by copper saddles. The ribs can slip harmlessly back and forth through the saddles as the two metals adjust separately to changes in temperature—from hot afternoon sun to chill night air.

copper saddle

The statue goes up

As the iron skeleton went up, coppersmiths brought the finished copper plates outside to the workyard. There each plate was hoisted up onto the skeleton, where workmen attached it to the horizontal and vertical iron ribs and bolted on the flat bar. Then they fastened the plate to its neighboring plates with a few temporary screws. Later, when the statue was rebuilt in America, more than 300,000 rivets would be inserted through the overlapping edges of the copper plates. For now, most of the carefully drilled rivet holes were left empty.

The first copper segment of the body was attached to the iron skeleton in a ceremony on October 24, 1881, when the American ambassador to France tapped a rivet into Liberty's big toe. Afterward the foot had to be removed temporarily so the ironworkers could continue building the skeleton.

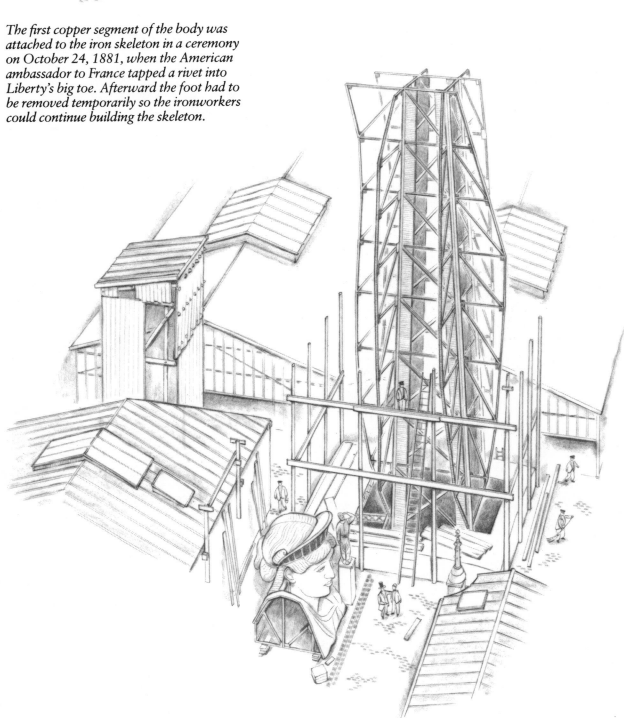

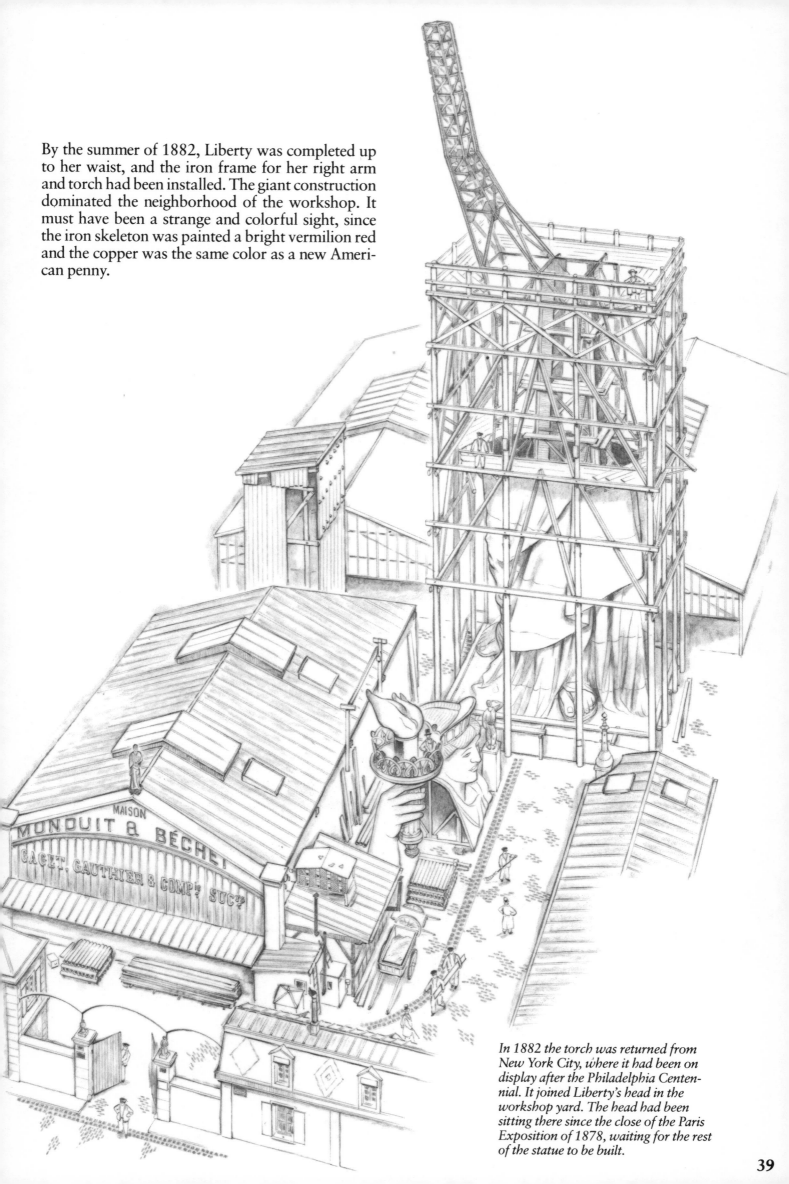

By the summer of 1882, Liberty was completed up to her waist, and the iron frame for her right arm and torch had been installed. The giant construction dominated the neighborhood of the workshop. It must have been a strange and colorful sight, since the iron skeleton was painted a bright vermilion red and the copper was the same color as a new American penny.

In 1882 the torch was returned from New York City, where it had been on display after the Philadelphia Centennial. It joined Liberty's head in the workshop yard. The head had been sitting there since the close of the Paris Exposition of 1878, waiting for the rest of the statue to be built.

39

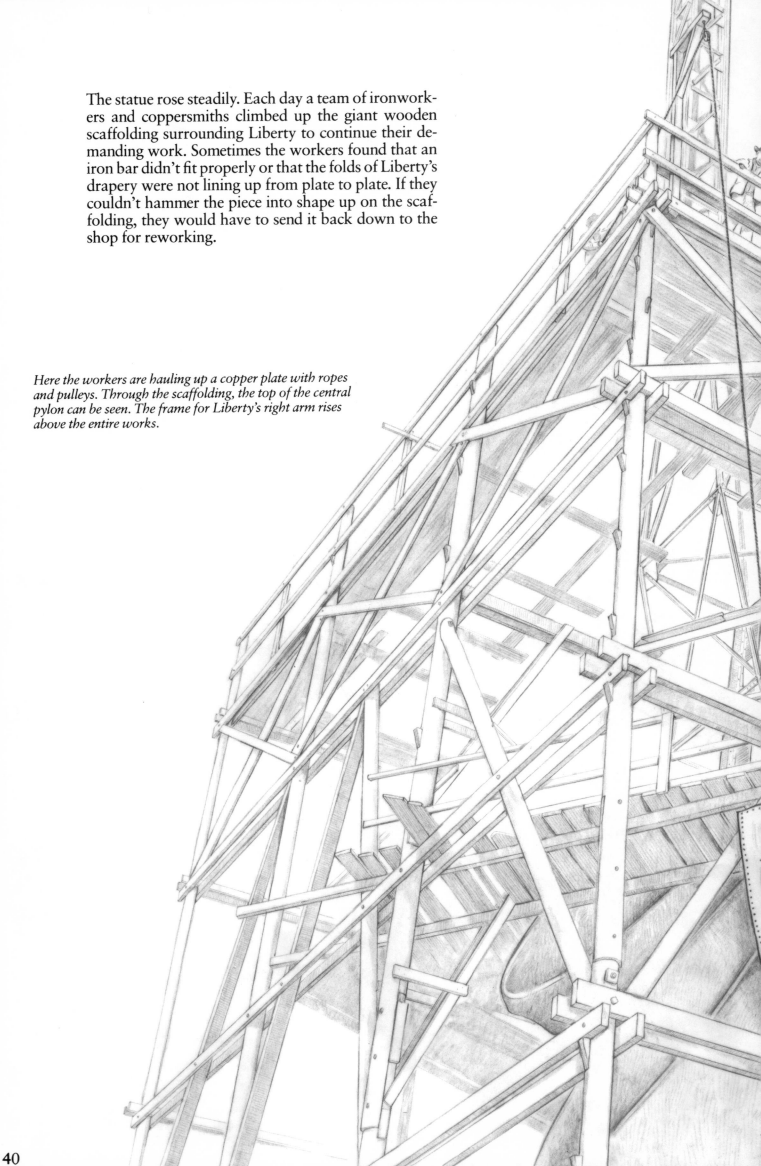

The statue rose steadily. Each day a team of ironworkers and coppersmiths climbed up the giant wooden scaffolding surrounding Liberty to continue their demanding work. Sometimes the workers found that an iron bar didn't fit properly or that the folds of Liberty's drapery were not lining up from plate to plate. If they couldn't hammer the piece into shape up on the scaffolding, they would have to send it back down to the shop for reworking.

Here the workers are hauling up a copper plate with ropes and pulleys. Through the scaffolding, the top of the central pylon can be seen. The frame for Liberty's right arm rises above the entire works.

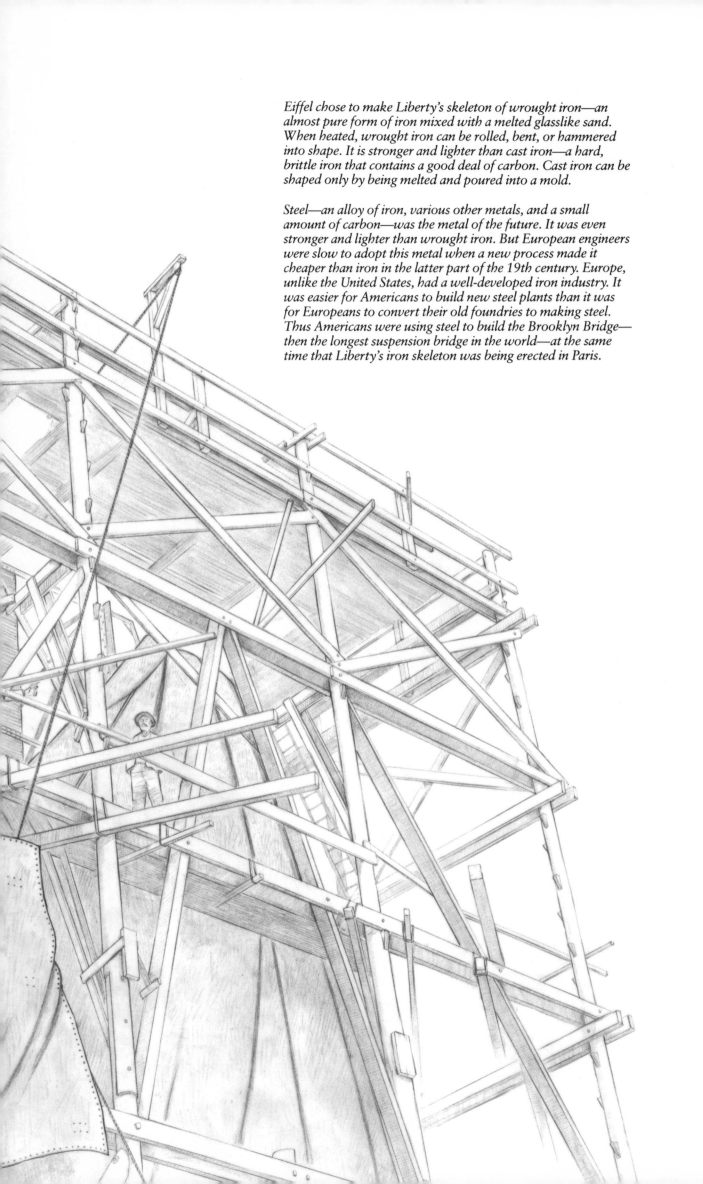

Eiffel chose to make Liberty's skeleton of wrought iron—an almost pure form of iron mixed with a melted glasslike sand. When heated, wrought iron can be rolled, bent, or hammered into shape. It is stronger and lighter than cast iron—a hard, brittle iron that contains a good deal of carbon. Cast iron can be shaped only by being melted and poured into a mold.

Steel—an alloy of iron, various other metals, and a small amount of carbon—was the metal of the future. It was even stronger and lighter than wrought iron. But European engineers were slow to adopt this metal when a new process made it cheaper than iron in the latter part of the 19th century. Europe, unlike the United States, had a well-developed iron industry. It was easier for Americans to build new steel plants than it was for Europeans to convert their old foundries to making steel. Thus Americans were using steel to build the Brooklyn Bridge— then the longest suspension bridge in the world—at the same time that Liberty's iron skeleton was being erected in Paris.

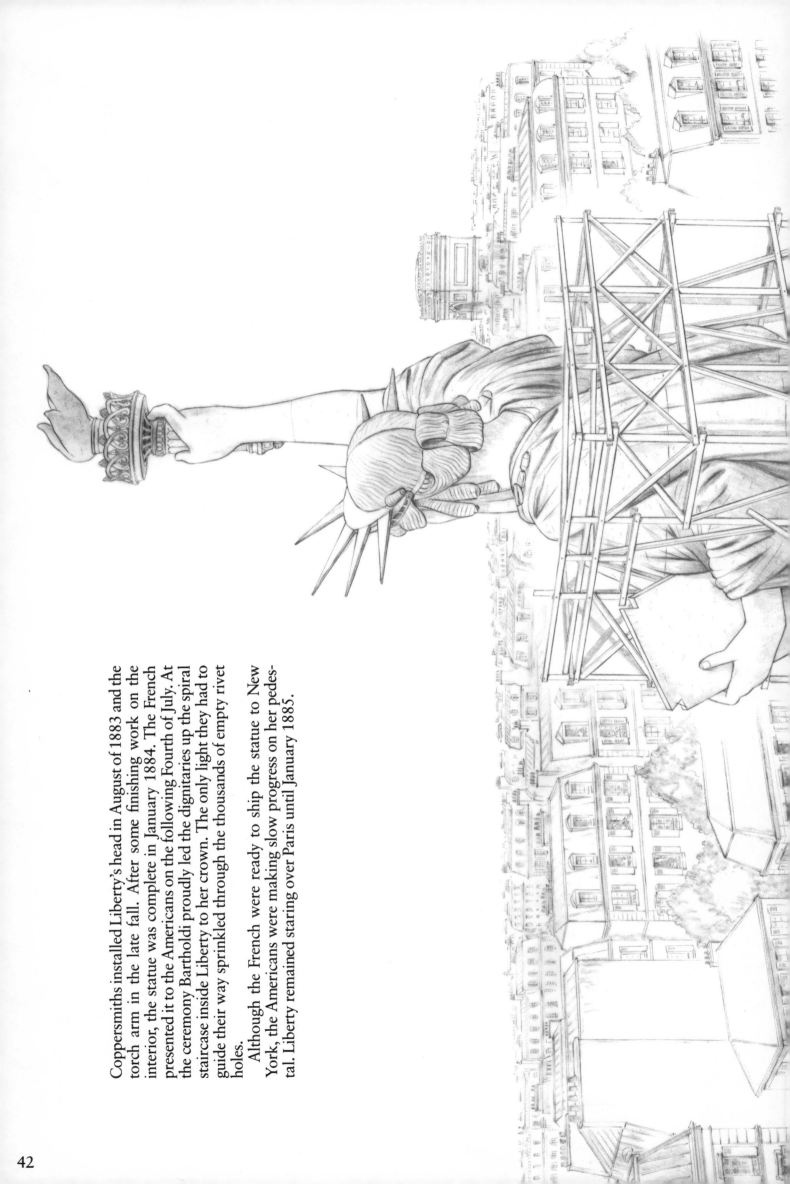

Coppersmiths installed Liberty's head in August of 1883 and the torch arm in the late fall. After some finishing work on the interior, the statue was complete in January 1884. The French presented it to the Americans on the following Fourth of July. At the ceremony Bartholdi proudly led the dignitaries up the spiral staircase inside Liberty to her crown. The only light they had to guide their way sprinkled through the thousands of empty rivet holes.

Although the French were ready to ship the statue to New York, the Americans were making slow progress on her pedestal. Liberty remained staring over Paris until January 1885.

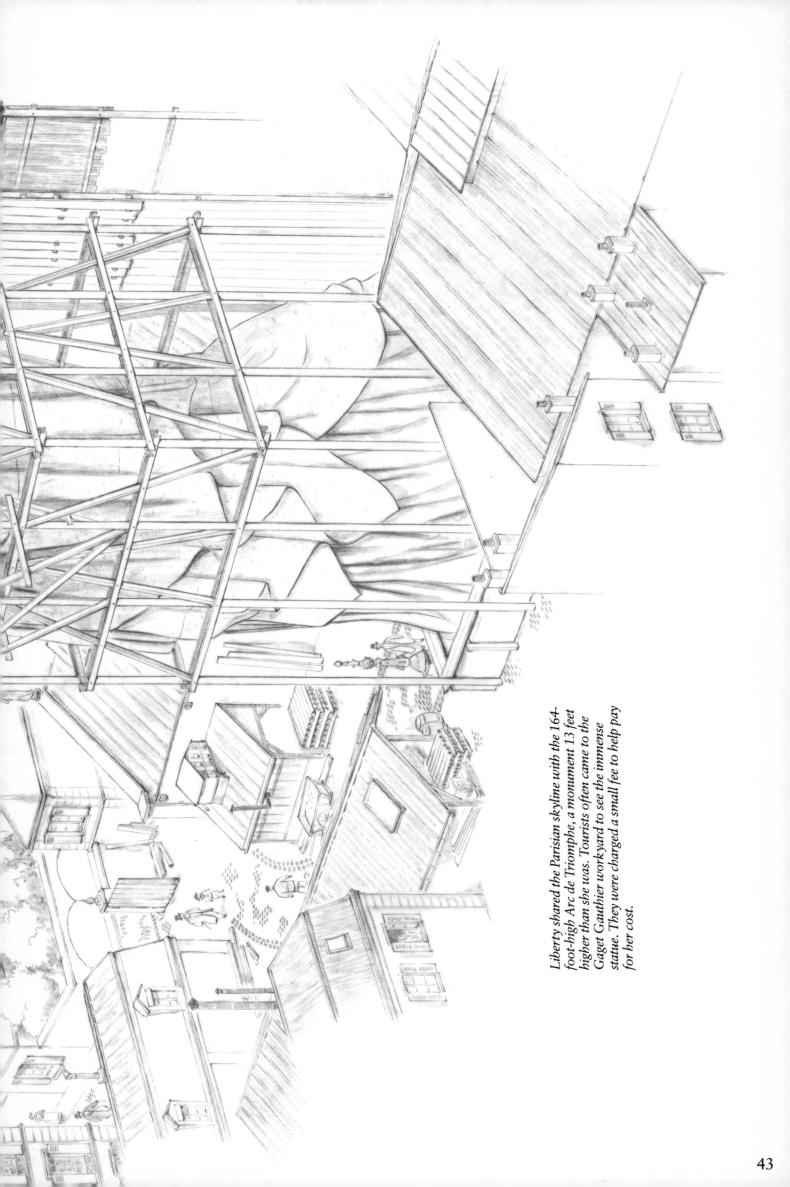

Liberty shared the Parisian skyline with the 164-foot-high Arc de Triomphe, a monument 13 feet higher than she was. Tourists often came to the Gaget Gauthier workyard to see the immense statue. They were charged a small fee to help pay for her cost.

43

Meanwhile in America . . .

The Americans finished building a foundation for Liberty's pedestal by August 1884. The work proved more difficult than General Charles P. Stone, the chief engineer, had expected. The site selected for Liberty was the parade ground within the walls of the army's Fort Wood on Bedloe's Island in New York harbor. Stone's first task was to excavate a great hole over 17 feet deep for the foundation. The digging went very slowly because there were old stone wells and bomb-proof shelters below the fort which had to be broken up and cleared away.

Starting at the bottom of the hole, Stone's workers then built a stepped pyramid of concrete—a mixture of cement, sand, and small stones. Solid except for a 27-foot-square shaftway in the center, the pyramid was the largest single mass of concrete ever made. It weighed more than 23,000 tons and was 65 feet high.

But this was only the foundation. On top of it would go Liberty's 89-foot-high pedestal—also made of concrete but faced with granite blocks. Richard Morris Hunt, the architect, had originally designed a pedestal that was 114 feet high. But the American Committee, the fund-raisers for the pedestal, were having such trouble that they asked Hunt to decrease the height to save money. They liked his second design much better and did not mind when its more intricate stonework pushed the cost of the pedestal even higher.

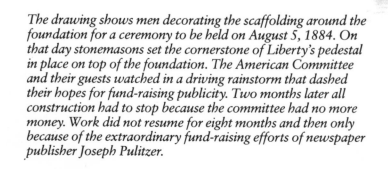

The drawing shows men decorating the scaffolding around the foundation for a ceremony to be held on August 5, 1884. On that day stonemasons set the cornerstone of Liberty's pedestal in place on top of the foundation. The American Committee and their guests watched in a driving rainstorm that dashed their hopes for fund-raising publicity. Two months later all construction had to stop because the committee had no more money. Work did not resume for eight months and then only because of the extraordinary fund-raising efforts of newspaper publisher Joseph Pulitzer.

The blocks of granite sitting at the base of the foundation were quarried on Leete's Island, Connecticut. Steam-powered derricks were mounted on the foundation to hoist the blocks and other building materials up to the pedestal builders.

Enthusiastic New Yorkers also welcomed the arrival of "Liberty Enlightening the World" with a parade up Broadway. Bands played, cannons roared, and thousands of spectators waved French and American flags.

The arrival of the *Isère*

Back in France, Bartholdi grew tired of waiting for the pedestal to be completed. Beginning in January 1885, his workmen started taking Liberty down. Each piece of shell and skeleton was carefully marked before it was detached from the statue. Liberty's parts were packed into more than 200 wooden crates, shipped by rail to the inland port of Rouen, and put aboard the *Isère*, a French naval vessel.

The glistening white ship set sail on May 21, 1885, and arrived in New York on June 19. As the flag-bedecked *Isère* steamed through New York harbor past the still-unfinished pedestal on Bedloe's Island, she was escorted by a magnificent naval parade.

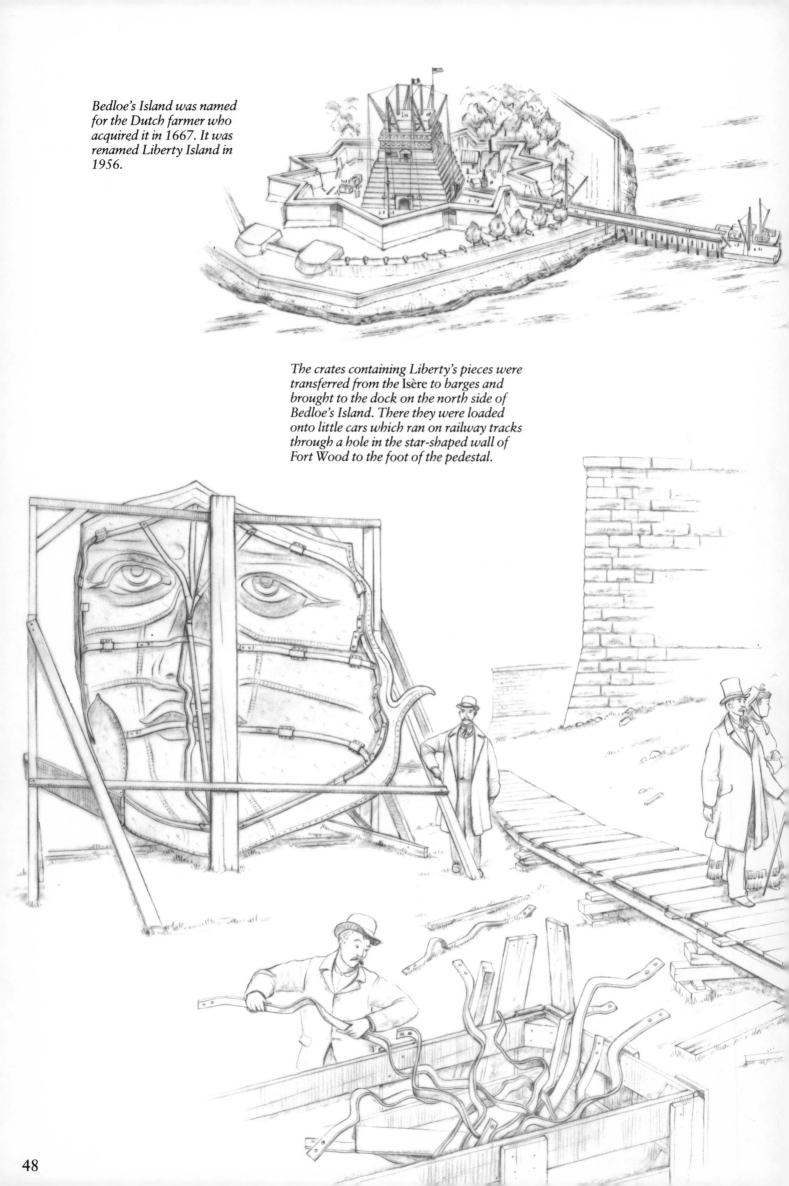

Bedloe's Island was named for the Dutch farmer who acquired it in 1667. It was renamed Liberty Island in 1956.

The crates containing Liberty's pieces were transferred from the Isère to barges and brought to the dock on the north side of Bedloe's Island. There they were loaded onto little cars which ran on railway tracks through a hole in the star-shaped wall of Fort Wood to the foot of the pedestal.

Liberty in pieces

Although the pedestal was not ready, workmen on Bedloe's Island unpacked some of Liberty's copper plates and reattached them to their iron ribs. The ribs kept the plates from losing their shape. When the statue was taken apart in Paris, each piece had been marked with a special number or letter, and adjoining edges were marked with identical symbols. These guided the Americans in putting the statue back together again.

As workers reassembled parts of the statue, they created a sort of outdoor sculpture studio. Visitors to the island could see Liberty's face propped up in the grass and could pose for their picture next to Liberty's giant toes and fingertips. When winter came, the pieces were stored away in sheds. The pedestal would not be ready for many more months.

The statue goes up again

Liberty's pedestal was finally completed in the spring of 1886. At the dedication ceremony on April 22, jubilant stonemasons threw a shower of silver coins into the mortar before they lowered the last block of granite into place.

Now the work of reconstructing Liberty could begin. Within two months the central pylon was in place and a steam-powered derrick was mounted on its top. Workers used the derrick to hoist up the secondary frame and then the rest of the ironwork and the copper plates.

To help the Americans reassemble the skeleton and shell, Bartholdi sent one of his own men from Paris. But even with his help, the workers often had trouble figuring out which piece went where. Some of the pieces had not been labeled correctly when the statue was taken down in Paris. The parts of the skeleton all looked very much alike. Sometimes the workers had to try as many as 20 pieces before they found the right one for a given spot.

top of
guy rods

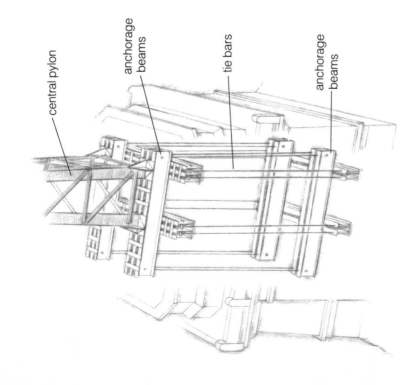

central pylon

anchorage
beams

tie bars

anchorage
beams

Liberty's skeleton is firmly anchored to two sets of crossed steel beams which are built right into the concrete walls of the pedestal. Tie bars connect the two sets of beams. The four legs of Liberty's central pylon are fastened to the top beams with three huge bolts apiece. For extra strength, eight long guy rods run from the middle of the pylon down to the top anchorage beams.

The bottom anchorage beams are set 55 feet down in the pedestal, the concrete of the pedestal is continuous with the concrete of the foundation, and the foundation is sunk over 17 feet into the ground. Thus the builders of the anchorage system could fairly say that if you wanted to overturn the statue, you would have to overturn the island itself.

During construction the skeleton was struck by lightning several times. No damage was done because the skeleton was grounded by four copper rods built into the pedestal and connected to metal plates buried in the moist earth beneath the foundation.

Bartholdi always wanted people to be able to go inside Liberty. When the statue was completed, visitors could climb an outside staircase to the base of the pedestal. Inside, a set of 167 stairs—and after 1908, an elevator—went up to the foot of the statue. From there, a double spiral staircase took the visitor up 171 more steps to Liberty's crown. Until 1916 the truly adventurous could also climb a 54-rung ladder from the shoulder to the torch. In later years Fort Wood was filled in with earth which covered most of the foundation. In the early 1970s a two-tiered building was added around Liberty's foundation to house the American Museum of Immigration.

A steam engine on the ground drove the hoisting cable for the derrick high atop Liberty's skeleton. The cable ran horizontally from a winch into the foundation and then up through the center of the foundation, the pedestal, and the pylon to the derrick—and then back down to the ground on the outside.

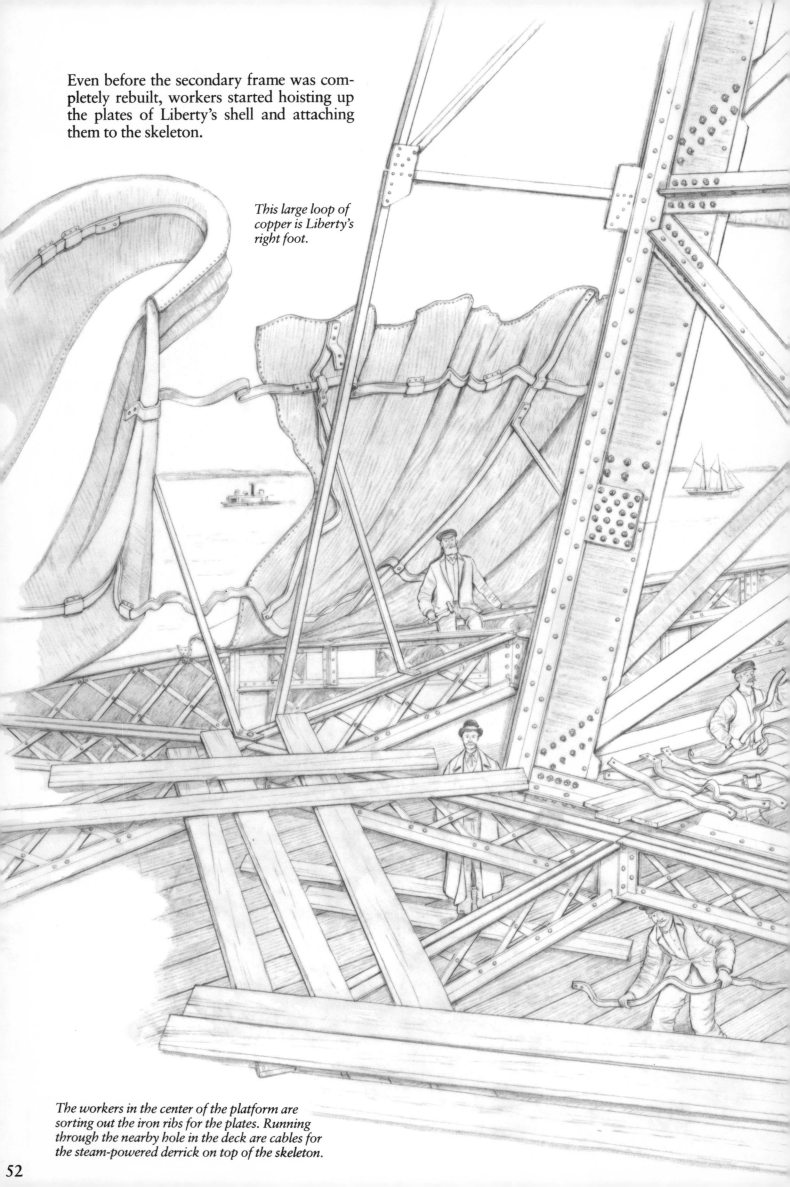

Even before the secondary frame was completely rebuilt, workers started hoisting up the plates of Liberty's shell and attaching them to the skeleton.

This large loop of copper is Liberty's right foot.

The workers in the center of the platform are sorting out the iron ribs for the plates. Running through the nearby hole in the deck are cables for the steam-powered derrick on top of the skeleton.

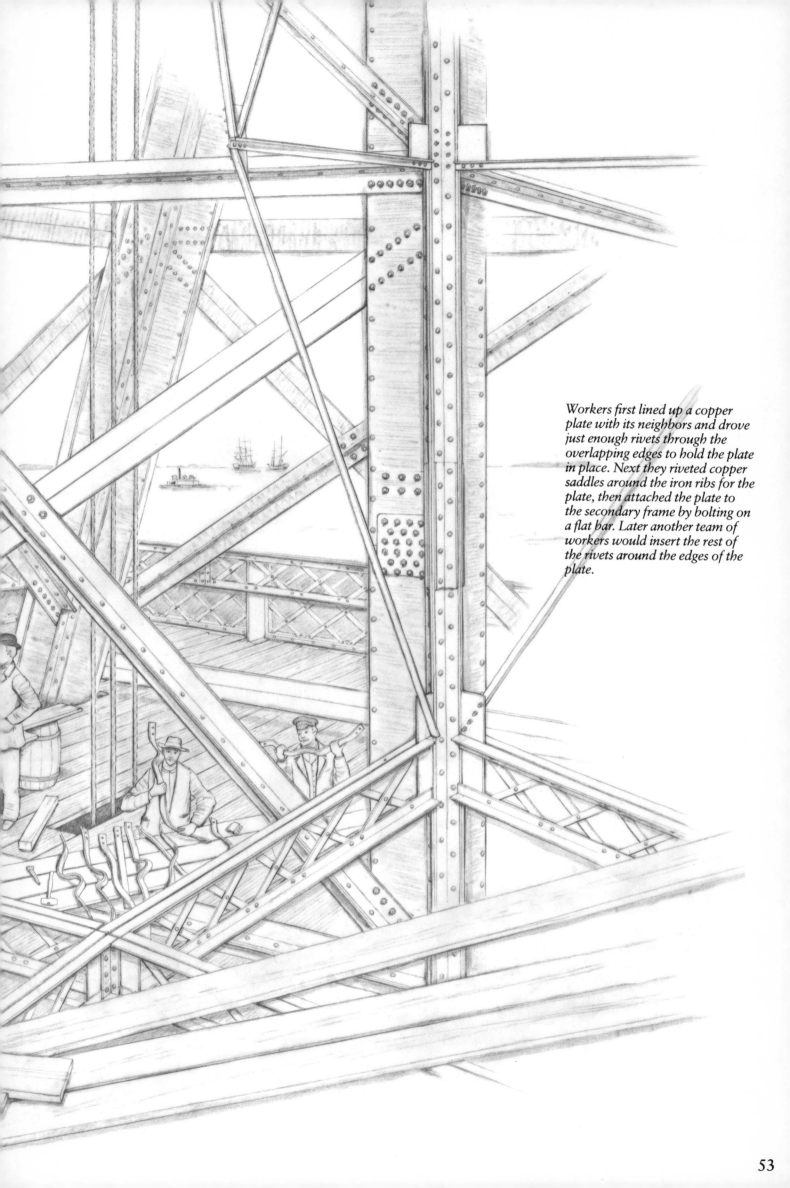

Workers first lined up a copper plate with its neighbors and drove just enough rivets through the overlapping edges to hold the plate in place. Next they riveted copper saddles around the iron ribs for the plate, then attached the plate to the secondary frame by bolting on a flat bar. Later another team of workers would insert the rest of the rivets around the edges of the plate.

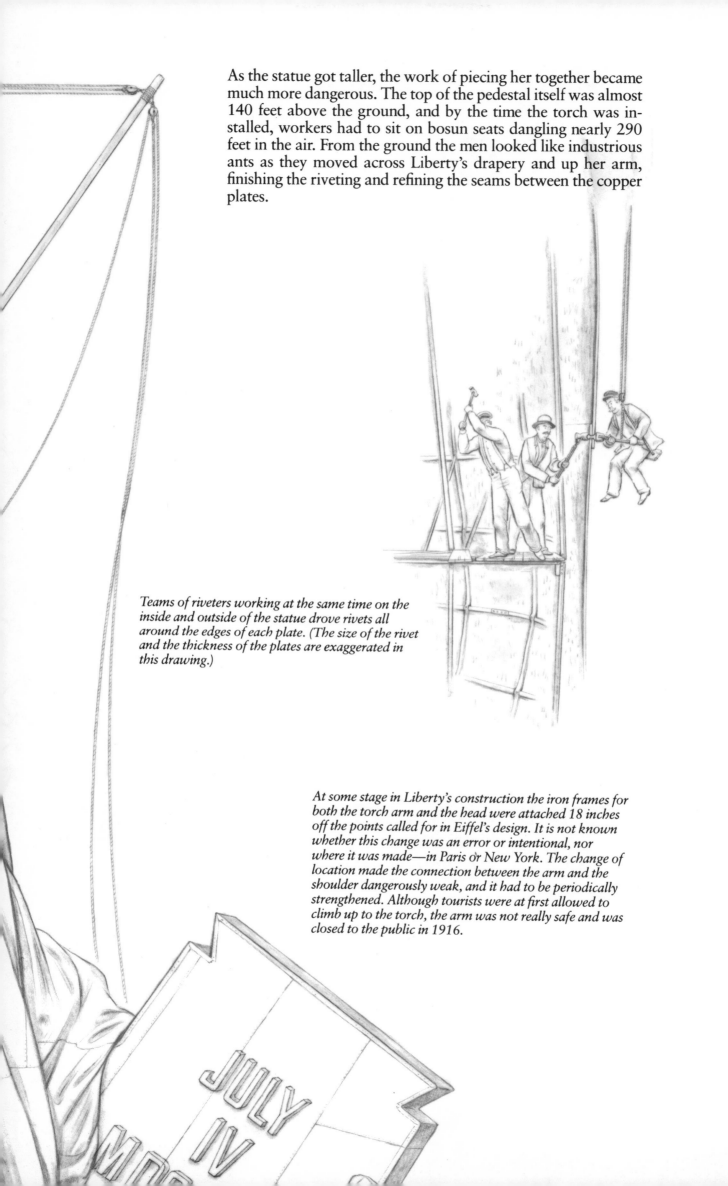

As the statue got taller, the work of piecing her together became much more dangerous. The top of the pedestal itself was almost 140 feet above the ground, and by the time the torch was installed, workers had to sit on bosun seats dangling nearly 290 feet in the air. From the ground the men looked like industrious ants as they moved across Liberty's drapery and up her arm, finishing the riveting and refining the seams between the copper plates.

Teams of riveters working at the same time on the inside and outside of the statue drove rivets all around the edges of each plate. (The size of the rivet and the thickness of the plates are exaggerated in this drawing.)

At some stage in Liberty's construction the iron frames for both the torch arm and the head were attached 18 inches off the points called for in Eiffel's design. It is not known whether this change was an error or intentional, nor where it was made—in Paris or New York. The change of location made the connection between the arm and the shoulder dangerously weak, and it had to be periodically strengthened. Although tourists were at first allowed to climb up to the torch, the arm was not really safe and was closed to the public in 1916.

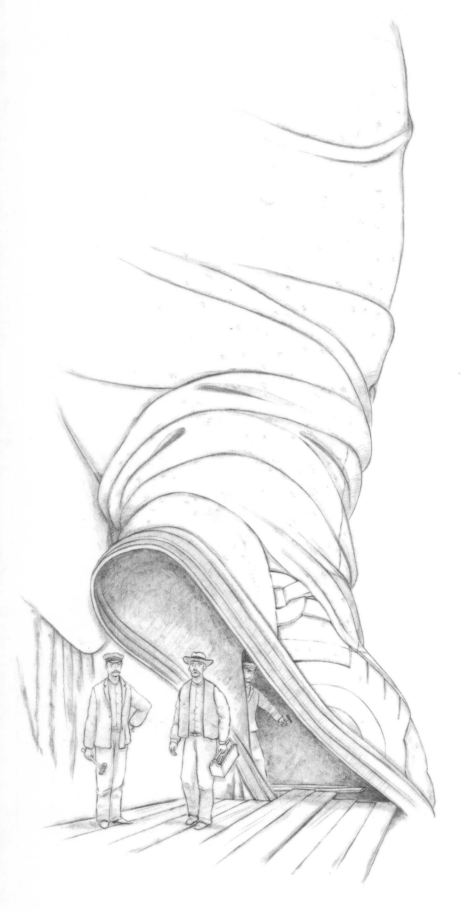

Liberty unveiled

"Liberty Enlightening the World" was unveiled on October 28, 1886, in one of the biggest celebrations New York had ever seen. Despite a drizzling rain and misty fog, more than 100,000 sightseers poured into the city. Auguste Bartholdi, President Grover Cleveland, Joseph Pulitzer, and members of the American Committee and the Franco-American Union stood together on the reviewing stand to watch a gala parade of 20,000 marchers in Manhattan.

Afterward there was a naval parade in honor of Liberty. New York's harbor filled with tugs, steamers, yachts, and ferries as a line of U.S. Navy warships escorted the President's yacht down the Hudson River to Bedloe's Island. There the official guests gathered on the speaker's platform to watch the unveiling.

The last piece of copper—the sole of Liberty's right sandal—was riveted into place on October 25, 1886. Throughout the building of the statue, workmen could enter and leave by way of this foot. Now the opening was sealed off in preparation for the unveiling.

Bartholdi was given the honor of unveiling his statue. He waited next to the pedestal, where a long cord led up to a French flag over Liberty's eyes. A young boy near the speaker's platform had the task of signaling the sculptor when it was time to drop the flag.

The unveiling was supposed to take place as soon as William Evarts, president of the American Committee, finished his dedication speech. Early on in his remarks, Evarts stopped for applause after a dramatic phrase. The excited boy mistook the pause for the end of the speech and eagerly waved to Bartholdi. The veil dropped; the band played; the watching ships let forth a blast of horns, whistles, and cannons; and church bells rang all over Brooklyn Heights and Manhattan. Evarts was unable to finish his speech.

When at last all was calm again, President Cleveland accepted the statue on behalf of the American people. "Liberty Enlightening the World"—or the Statue of Liberty, as she has always been popularly known—was now home.

Liberty's unveiling was also celebrated with a huge fireworks display. It was scheduled to take place the same day but had to be postponed four nights because of rain. The Americans had cut two rows of round windows in the copper flame of Liberty's torch and had installed a powerful electric lamp inside. As the fireworks went off, Liberty's torch was lit for the first time.

On the night of the fireworks display, Liberty's shell was reddish-brown in color. Thirty years later it was blue-green. When copper is exposed to damp air for a long time, it slowly becomes coated with a green film, called patina. The patina protects the metal from further corrosion.

In 1885 Americans living in Paris donated a ¼-size bronze replica of Liberty to the people of Paris as a return gesture of friendship. The statue stands today at the end of the Ile des Cygnes in the Seine River, not far from the Eiffel Tower.

100 years of Liberty

After the unveiling, the Statue of Liberty soon became one of America's most powerful symbols. Known to people around the world as a stirring monument to independence, she more than fulfilled Bartholdi and Laboulaye's dream.

But Liberty did not fare so well as an enduring structure. Years of inadequate care took their toll. In the early 1980s Liberty was found to have serious structural problems. Almost the entire network of iron ribs and flat bars inside the statue had become corroded because of water seeping in around windows in the torch and through seams and rivet holes in the copper shell. A full-scale restoration was needed.

Now Liberty has new ribs and flat bars of stainless steel. Her torch has been sculpted anew and the flame plated with gold. The weak connection between the torch arm and the shoulder has been thoroughly reinforced. Improvements have been made inside the pedestal and the statue itself so that tourists can see the magnificent framework and anchoring system more clearly.

The work of the restorers—a team of American and French architects, engineers, and artisans—has made the statue better than new. Thanks to their efforts, Bartholdi's colossus will continue to inspire the love of liberty in the hearts of many generations to come.

Seven famous colossal statues drawn to the same scale so that their heights can be compared.

"Saint Charles Borromeo, Arona, Italy, 1697, Repoussé copper, 76 ft.

"The Great Sphinx," Giza, Egypt, c. 2550 B.C., Limestone, 66 ft.

"The Great Buddha," Kamakura, Japan, 1252, Bronze, 42 ft.

Abraham Lincoln, Lincoln Memorial, Washington, D.C., U.S.A., 1922, Marble, 19 ft.

Michelangelo's "David," Florence, Italy, 1504, Marble, 14 ft.

Statistics for the Statue of Liberty

Base of foundation to torch	305 ft. 1 in.
Base of statue to torch	151 ft. 1 in.
Heel to top of head	111 ft. 1 in.
Height of pedestal	89 ft.
Height of foundation	65 ft.
Length of torch	21 ft.
Length of right arm	42 ft.
Greatest thickness of right arm	12 ft.
Longest ray in crown	11 ft. 6 in.
Head from chin to top	17 ft. 3 in.
Head from ear to ear	10 ft.
Distance across eye	2 ft. 6 in.
Length of nose	4 ft. 6 in.
Width of mouth	3 ft.
Length of hand	16 ft. 5 in.
Index finger	7 ft. 11 in.
Size of fingernail	13 in. x 10 in.
Height of tablet	23 ft. 7 in.
Greatest thickness of waist	35 ft.
Thickness of copper shell	3/32 in.
Number of copper plates	350
Steps in statue	171
Weight of copper in statue	100 tons
Weight of skeleton	125 tons
Total weight of statue	225 tons

Liberty's pedestal and foundation, Concrete and granite, 154 ft. Statue, pedestal, and foundation combined, 305 ft.

"Motherland," Volgograd, U.S.S.R., 1967, Reinforced concrete, 270 ft.

"Liberty Enlightening the World," New York City, U.S.A., 1886, Repoussé copper, 151 ft.

ABOUT THE AUTHOR

Mary J. Shapiro's research for her first book, *A Picture History of the Brooklyn Bridge,* helped prepare her for writing about the Statue of Liberty: What she learned about nineteenth-century engineering enabled her to understand Liberty's ingenious design. Mrs. Shapiro has also written two walking-tour guides to Manhattan, illustrated with her own photographs and drawings, and is currently working on a picture history of Ellis Island. She received a B.A. degree in art from Manhattanville College and an M.F.A. in film from New York University. She lives in New York City with her husband, Barry, and her two sons, Michael and Eben.

ABOUT THE ILLUSTRATOR

Huck Scarry's talent for conveying technical information through lively pictures has previously been demonstrated in a number of sketchbooks and science books. He is the author-illustrator of nine books on transport, including *On Wheels* and *Balloon Trip: A Sketchbook;* a young readers' encyclopedia entitled *Our Earth;* and *My First Picture Dictionary.* Mr. Scarry has lived in Switzerland since he was fifteen, when his family moved there from Connecticut. He studied art there and in Florence and Paris. At present he, his wife, Marlis, and his daughters, Fiona and Olympia, live in Geneva.